"These poems are stories built from what the eye photographed and the heart carried in knapsacks across a lifetime. This is Margaret Randall's personal history threaded by dwellings. She writes, 'I am writing / it all down, putting it in books / where it stays safe and willing.' From the heights of a life lived deeply, she writes what she has learned as an artist activist. Home is not something inherited, but an act as creative as writing a poem. This book is a homecoming. I celebrate with you."

— Sandra Cisneros, author of *Woman Without Shame*

"In these fraught times, as we shelter in places and spaces that ultimately cannot keep us safe, as we witness and grieve the violations that have increasingly made the Earth an uninhabitable home for the most vulnerable in our human and planetary family—our sister rivers and our brother trees—we ache for what homes stories and poems can provide us, the big tables they construct in our imaginations where all are welcomed. Margaret Randall has long been providing that circle of connection and compassion through her essays, stories, and the poetry of her person. Hers has always been a moral and compassionate imagination. Here in this latest collection of poems, *Home*, she meditates on all the permutations of that word, what is a home, how do we make a house a home, what homes can we make where everyone belongs, what memories do we bring that shelter us going forward. Her voice is the master-builder we need as we rebuild our communities and our lives as a people. *Mi casa, su casa,* we say, and these poems provide us all with a space to call home."

— Julia Alvarez, author of *In the Time of the Butterflies,*
How the García Girls Lost Their Accents, and
The Woman I Kept to Myself

"I can't think of a better writer to explore the concept of home through poetry than Margaret Randall. Over the years she has fought to establish households in New York City, Mexico City, Cuba, Nicaragua, and finally Albuquerque. She was actually kept from returning home to the United States in 1984 under the McCarren-Walter Act. Despite such harassment, she has always remained ready to uncover and to join new struggles. Randall's visioning and deft phrasing are entirely unique, and the questions that emerge from reading *Home* are priceless: Aren't the places that we call home often lands that have been seized from their native inhabitants? Is our near future meant to be entirely nomadic? Is home a truly eternal (prism-like) space that we must establish and hold beyond our physical bodies?"

— Cedar Sigo, author of *Stranger in Town*

"From the plight of the homeless to the magnificence of Chaco Canyon, Margaret Randall surveys the meanings of 'home' in all its manifestations. This is a marvelous book, featuring the combination of sensitivity, insight, historical knowledge, and strength we have come to expect from Randall's work."

— David Stephen Calonne, author of
The Beats in Mexico

"In this engrossing collection, Randall's poems enter home spaces that are quiet as her darkroom and yet move across time and space 'like wind / in your hair.' These homes are made of adobe and memory, sandstone and 'unwanted secrets,' 'Worries like overripe berries.' They offer rich imagery that seeks in architectural structure 'the real hunger of living.' 'Home speaks a new language' in this volume, becomes an abundant metaphor—'a cavern of heartbeats.' A major poet of our age has come home here to 'nest / and stretch,' but also to continue to fling herself and her vision across 'vistas / of the knowable world' that have long fueled Randall's remarkable poetic legacy."

— Ruth Salvaggio, author of
Hearing Sappho in New Orleans

Home

Selected works by Margaret Randall

Poems:
Time's Language II: Selected Poems 2019-2023
Vertigo of Risk
Stormclouds Like Unkept Promises
Out of Violence into Poetry
Starfish on a Beach: The Pandemic Poems
Time's Language: Selected Poems 1959-2018
As If the Empty Chair / Como si la silla vacía
The Rhizome as a Field of Broken Bones
About Little Charlie Lindbergh
She Becomes Time
The Morning After: Poems & Prose in a Post-Truth World

Nonfiction:
Artists in My Life
Thinking about Thinking
I Never Left Home: Poet, Feminist, Revolutionary
My Life in 100 Objects
Che on My Mind
More Than Things
Haydée Santamaría: She Led by Transgression
Exporting Revolution: Cuba's Global Solidarity

Home

poems

Margaret Randall

Casa Urraca Press
ABIQUIÚ

Cover photograph by Barbara Byers.
Author photograph by Magdalena Lily McCarson.
Set in Nobel and Odile.

26 25 24 23   1 2 3 4 5 6 7

First edition

ISBN 978-1-956375-30-5

CASA URRACA PRESS

an imprint of Casa Urraca, Ltd.
PO Box 1119
Abiquiú, New Mexico 87510
casaurracapress.com

This book is for Ximena.

Contents

These poems, all written in a flood of experience, dream, notetaking, and revision from mid-2021 to the end of the following year, explore the notion of home from multiple angles. They move through my own memories and stories others have told me, to include testimony by those who suffer homelessness, a condition that—to our shame—has acquired overwhelming proportions. In an age of unsettling displacement and monstrous migrations, home can be elusive. Ultimately, for many it is what we carry within us rather than a geographical place.

Four of these poems first appeared, in Spanish translation, in *Esteros*, Quito, Ecuador. Several have been accepted for *50*.

"The outrider rides the edge—parallel to the
mainstream, is the shadow to the mainstream,
is the consciousness or soul of the mainstream
whether it recognizes its existence or not. It cannot
be co-opted; it cannot be bought."
                                        —*Anne Waldman*

"It is not just that we expound story and poetry, but
we think it and it thinks us back."
                                        —*Sherwin Bitsui*

"As globalization draws us together, and
industrialization and human population pressures
take their toll on natural habitats, as species of
plants and animals flicker and are snuffed from
the earth, it may be worthwhile to ask whether
an ethnocentric view of human beings as a
species independent from others underpins our
exploitation of natural resources and sets into
motion dire consequences."
                                        —*Forrest Gander*

All three quotations are from *New Weathers: Poetics
from the Naropa Archive*, edited by Anne Waldman
and Emma Gomis. New York: Nighboat Books, 2022.

Home

This Home on My Back

For all those who have had to flee political repression

Some people live in the same house
their whole lives. Mother may
make a brief hospital detour
then bring baby back to rooms
whose shapes she's known all hers.

They will grow, raise their families
and die between those walls.
Trees they helped plant when young
now tower above its roofline,
still depositing new seed upon the ground.

My houses embrace me after accidental
journeys. I sometimes had to exit fast
or take a dangerous route, learning
the words *underground* and *clandestine*
in languages I didn't know.

My gardens, when I could plant them,
grew annuals not perennials,
knowing I might have to leave
before I could encourage their return
another season.

In my attic there is no cedar-lined chest
storing remnants of forebears' lives,
no family albums with photos
arranged in chronological memory
or books my mother's mother read to her.

My children didn't know
their grandparents,
had no aunts and uncles taking them
to the park, cousins tossing them
a ball or revealing family secrets.

I've carried my life from country
to country in small knapsacks
on my back, crossed borders with
choked breath, hoping ominous uniforms
would look the other way.

The food I cook isn't traditional
but learned in each new place,
glimmers of solidarity trading hands
over stoves that use whatever fuel
is to be had.

Age, a steady love, and this era
of slowing rhythms
make their own home for me now,
one in which all those
imagined disappear.

And oh, but the people we've met
along the way, the dreams
and ideas and poems they've
given us, the justice reflected
in their eyes!

The home I bequeath my children
and grandchildren isn't made
of stone or brick but moves like wind
in your hair, carrying its energy
across all borders into future time.

Home as Oxymoron

From outside looking in
every house might be
called a home.

But if the child is frightened
into submission she is
only there until she can escape.

If forced to parent her parents
she may not remember
childhood.

If he was told to be a man
he may grow up to be
a brutal one.

When family becomes cult
home is an oxymoron
dangerously hoarded.

To become a real home, it
must earn its name
in reciprocity and love.

Rooms

When the rooms of a house
bicker with one another
seasonal winds may be at fault.

Kitchen wants to gather us
at a round table, no seat
at the head, no privilege.

Bedroom has seen enough to write
a thriller, secrets that may
lose their allure in time.

Bathroom is always ill, its
rituals mundane,
repetitive and dull.

No one pays attention to entry,
liminal space
except in the far north

where Mud Room asks you
to remove your shoes
and scarf, hang your coat

on a peg that supports all
manner of outerwear
known to rain and storm.

Here our studios are the rooms
with most to say
that speak the loudest.

This is where life chooses silence,
then leaps into passionate gear,
making our house a home.

The Life We Create and Recreate

Our home is shaped like a hand
reaching for the temperature
of another hand
when all scores are tallied.

This room traces the imprint
of our bodies growing
old in the life
we create and recreate.

That one cradles our future,
then laughs and shelters it
from prying
or curious eyes.

The place where our minds wander
is supported by floorboards
that creak
and moan beneath our feet.

A chair, bearing the impression
of your pain and my stillness
blurs its reflection
on any winter day.

Our home is shaped like a petal
of moonflower showing
its pale face
in the richness of night.

The Shame No Wearable Can Erase

This house wears a beige trench coat,
the kind with upturned collar
and loosely knotted belt
showing a lean and hungry body, revolver
holstered at the ready.

A Maasai hut, constructed of cow dung
and anthill soil, wraps the vivid red
of a Sears blanket above its loincloth
as it goes in search of the trail
of lion scent.

In the far north, an ice-block igloo
protects itself against the cold
with whale blubber, seal skins and a parka
guaranteed by L.L. Bean to withstand
up to fifty degrees below.

Men cover the heads and bodies of
their fundamentalist homes
in hair or wig or heavy cloth, possession
nine-tenths of the law. The home cries
silent obedience.

A starter home buys cotton sundresses
each spring, ruffle and flounce,
hasn't yet learned more elegant outfits
straddle the seasons
and remain in fashion.

The old commune shopped *vintage* when
vintage and *used* meant the same.
Now *used* has raised its margin of profit
and *vintage* is the Stradivarius
only a virtuoso can afford.

The rooms added to this house
bare their midriffs in summer
but cover their windows
with lace curtains replacing truth
with memory's lies.

An expensive retreat in its gated community
flaunts jewels and ostentatious furs,
Jimmy Choo heels and
the $5000 evening bag:
tarnished as it is glamorous.

A penthouse dons the most expensive suit,
imported Italian serge and tailoring
only mega bucks can buy, except when it
settles on a personal trademark:
turtleneck, black.

Any one of the rent-controlled apartments
in these projects, elevator
reeking of piss, would rather its children
wear school uniforms
than see its men in prison green.

I know a house where overalls hide a body
afraid of being touched,
although the latest shoes and bags
bring a sense of self
it can't resist.

My own home wears Levi's and a black shirt,
short sleeved in summer, long in winter,
rarely changes for any occasion.
It is statement, not necessity,
message rather than style.

Those who have no home
shuffle through the streets
in ragged blankets or whatever they can find.
Style loses its importance
when all it covers is need.

Each house appears in clothes
designed to do their best
against the demands of industry,
transformation, or
the shame no wearable can erase.

Home Is Where the Heart Is

Home is where the heart is
the sampler tells us:
a catchy phrase that keeps us
surface satisfied.

But when the heart
is shattered
by hate, bigotry, violence
or lies,

it is everywhere and nowhere,
trying in vain
to reassemble itself
on shaky terrain.

Myths abound about that tireless
muscle, and we are led
to believe our emotions
really do live there.

We can feel it palpitating
beneath the breastbone,
moving to the rhythms
of learned endurance.

Truth is, we must create home
anew each morning,
tuck it into bed each night,
nurture it in our desire.

Home is where the heart is only
when our coordinates
are clear and we search
in the four directions:

east, west, north, and south.
Then heart takes possibility
into account, often making home
from nothing

but two sets of weary eyes
meeting across
a vast emptiness, two mouths
igniting possibility.

The Great Houses, Chaco[1]

For my grandson, Eli Bickford

We call it the Menefee formation,
peach-colored sandstone
rising in billowing benches,
shouldering eighty million years.

Reflecting all that summer sun,
its bulk and crevices dance
in our eyes, imposing monument
upon a land that holds its secrets close.

Beside them, the great houses
hewn from this rock
bear no evidence anyone lived
in their hundreds of small dark rooms.

No blackened walls, few hearths
from cooking fires confirming
daily life, no middens ripe
with household debris.

[1] I've visited Chaco Canyon many times over the
years, but a recent visit immediately after viewing
Anna Sofaer's 1999 film *The Mystery of Chaco Canyon*
provided me with a deeper understanding of the site
that is reflected in this poem.

This is an intimate grandeur
immense as the fingertips
of two lovers meeting in a city
neither knows.

Living rock dies in these chiseled blocks
yet lives in another dimension,
the liminal space time's transition
sets before us.

The great kivas are roofless now.
Only ghosts dance within,
perpetuating their meaning,
guarding their secrets.

Mounds of broken pottery
tell stories of offerings
made in rituals hidden
beyond our consciousness.

Built on this hardscrabble earth,
standing four or five stories
tall, their broken silhouettes
weather seasons and centuries.

Even at midday, long shadows pass
in angular movement
framing windows of sky, bursts of cloud
against a depth of blue.

Traveling from the four directions,
the people found this center,
hauled rock and timber to align
the cosmos in this place.

For generations they recorded cycles
of sun and moon, traced
an accurate astronomical signature
in ceremonial memory.

I almost close my eyes and a dish-
shaped moon becomes
lunar repetition moving in tandem
across the night.

I imagine an adolescent girl, perhaps
thirteen or fourteen, walking
the Great North Road from her people
far to the south.

Her garment is loose, her hair black
and braided. She carries
knowledge and intention
to this land on which

every eighteen-and-a-half-year cycle
the moon casts a dagger of light:
its perfect image piercing the spiral
etched on rock.

Today's celestial body shines upon
a barren and desolate landscape,
offering the same light
it did back then.

The girl still walks through time,
one step before another,
measuring where we've been
and where we have yet to go.

Leaving no written language,
architecture and location
is their script. Past meets future
in the old man's eyes

as he tells us: *parts of that story*
aren't meant to be told,
those parts where the power
gleaned by some

may have caused certain things
to happen, wrong turns
to be taken or mistakes that
needn't be repeated.

Their knowledge may have
been too great, he says,
and something changed,
went bad.

Knowing we do not need to know
it all may seem a misstep of faith
but things were different then.
They faced the same uncertainty

we battle today but their imaginations
took root in a landscape
whose voices spoke to them.
They listened.

Nothing but Need at Their Side

They tell great stories about their childhood homes:
hers on the prominent shore of a placid lake
surrounded by other monied families, his smaller one
nurtured by his teacher parents. He brought the politics
they embody to the life they share.

Honoring gay friends who couldn't marry back then,
they never did so either. Their son bears
her surname because, why not? The children
whose families shared their floorspace and dreams
were his brothers and sisters.

As young professors they lived in an old three-story
collective house, shared kitchen, cooked meals
together, navigated its communal spaces.
They parented intentionally and laughed
when friends asked about their way of life.

The commune was always their goal, and they lived
that goal beyond the walls that held them
city to city as they grew in their professions,
moved from one college town to another until
they settled under this desert sun.

Their one-family home is filled with art from
the Navajo family she studied for decades,
is lined with his books on Brazil's economy.
It stretched to make five years of room
for the first Begay to go beyond high school,

an old friend who needed a roof for years
and now their son, his wife and child,
because extended family is also where
he feels comfortable and what he wants
his son to inherit.

Which is why we are bereft of words when
they tell us they are moving
to *assisted living*, eldercare with a *memory unit*
in case they forget how they used to live
and what it meant.

It has a beautiful view of the mountains, she
explains, *and chances are one of us*
will need the help as we grow older.
Hiding our tears, we take a last look around,
smile and nod our heads,

trying to imagine *assisted living* as a new kind
of commune, capitalism's answer to human
frailty for those who have the means
while others try to survive on streets
with nothing but pain in their hands.

A Different Language

My curiosity sometimes retreats
to decades before my birth
and I watch a distant European relative
turn down an unfamiliar street.

This prevents her from running
into the man she married,
alters her life completely, thus
cancelling or replacing mine.

One small difference, a day that turned
stormy rather than bright,
accidents or choices made by those
we never knew.

A desire to speak silenced by sudden
shame. A piece of music perfectly
performed, leading to an outcome
challenging history.

The rogue gene, brazen decision,
fear hiding in plain sight
or courage rising on a tide
that switches direction in the night.

The insult that cannot be forgotten,
a child lost at war's end, one face
missing or added
in the family photograph.

Good fortune embraced her for a while,
then didn't. He was said to have
a way with women until his wife
chose death rather than one more day.

She became the woman she always
knew she was. He refused
to give in to his entitlement, forfeited
confidence to social equanimity.

The storm of the century, the one
they called perfect. Famine
eroding teeth and muscle, generosity
or arrogance stealing the scene.

Ordinary or extraordinary events
in ordinary lives. The lie
that prospered or a truth
that could not speak its name.

Any one of those choices allowed,
provoked, stumbled upon
this future that is me. And I cannot
but wonder about another story,

one in which I was born somewhere
else, spoke a different language,
am taller, healthier, darker of skin
or don't exist at all.

Their Houses

Their houses still pretend
to be their homes,
price of a ticket to explore
rooms cordoned off
to excessive curiosity.
And we tickle an illusion
of how they lived.

I could barely stand in
Elizabeth Cady's
bedroom, couldn't
imagine a mattress
large enough to hold
her solid bulk, the desk
that framed her passion.

Elvis's mansion displays
the pomp and glitter
needed to hide
the insecurity
beneath his swivel-
hipped gyrations
and magnificent voice.

Searching for the General's
final home
in a northern field
where she was free,
I found no historic evidence,
no sign proclaiming
Harriet Tubman Lived Here.

O'Keeffe's spartan rooms
give us a low bench here,
sun-bleached cow skull
there, tell us loud and clear
we may not cross
the line she drew
while alive.

Frida, always more flamboyant,
hid her withered leg
but bared
a vibrant heart
and Plaster of Paris bodice.
Her ashes greet us from
the pillow where she died.

Ho Chi Minh resided
in two rooms
even when president,
had to walk a block
to use a bathroom.
His modesty
still inspires.

Mandela returned
from his years
in prison to the same
simple house
on the same street
where he lived
before that arduous test.

And there's Queen Elizabeth II,
longest reigning monarch
in a nation where some
resent her palaces
while many still feel
their own lives brightened
by the pomp of royalty.

Some houses of those
we admire from afar
woo us with their books
or copper kitchen pots:
Hemingway's typewriter,
the post-it notes
stuck to Leonora's stove.

The houses we visit
hoping to inhale
the air our idols breathed,
the lives they lived,
are only absent
of the men and women
who called them home.

Mexico Trembles

September 19, 1985: the nation
shuddered at its root,
leaving ten thousand dead.

Fault lines broke apart, raising
their arms in wild disarray,
tectonic plates in cacophony.

The earth trembled with a violence
still felt today, mirroring
its promise of terror.

September 19, 2017, it happened again.
Same date and we gasped
as we mouthed the word *coincidence*.

Then September 19, 2022, the familiar
day, time, event—as if earthquakes
are telling us they read calendars.

The small animal turned loose
in my question
snickers as I try to sleep.

Is it something about September or
its nineteenth day, something ominous
lodged beneath earth's fragile skin?

Where will superstition take us
in this time when fantasy
beckons and fables disappear

on a bed of broken mirrors
as they try to entice us
away from what we know for sure?

Before Nature Kicked in His Door

He built with attention to nature's whims:
shear walls, cross braces, diaphragms
and movement-resisting frames to calm
the effects of earth whenever she trembled
threatening to attack his home.

Nothing was too much. He started with a
strong foundation, tiny motion sensors
throughout and reinforced concrete
to withstand the fury of hurricanes.
His windows were shatter-proof glass

and when that window glass started to fog
or a jagged crack opened in a supporting
wall, moving from ceiling to floor and
a coat of paint failed to stop the damage
spreading from room to room,

he researched the latest remedies, most
expensive fixes—money no problem
for him. He paid his workmen more
than the going rate, though offered them
no water, refused them restroom relief.

His house is immune to fire and flood,
displays the latest innovations in
precaution, safety, resistance. He
called on experts, spared no expense
in planning or execution.

Mid-summer, with garden parties in
bloom, he began to notice spots
of moisture in a closet, slow spread
of mold like dark petals of a poison
flower growing beneath an eave.

In winter a forest of termites made
their home in hardwood panels
faster than he could attack them
with injections of kerosene in the tunnels
where they hid to escape his ire.

Before nature kicked in his door, rotted
half his roof, ate beams and targeted
rare first editions with promises of fixes
he knew were lies, he gave up
and moved to a better neighborhood.

The gated community is guarded by a
24/7 contingent of guards wielding
submachineguns who require IDs
from every visitor and keep anyone
out who cannot prove they belong.

In bad weather the doorman tips
a cap and brings his Mercedes
to the door. Packages arrive via
the service elevator. No one intrudes
on his precious time.

No plague can get to him with every
surface disinfected by daily
contingents of workers wearing
N95 masks, who wash their rough
hands until they crack and bleed.

He can relax inside this fortress
where no one enters or leaves.
Meals arrive pre-treated and tested.
He cannot hear disturbance
in the streets or cries of those in need.

He can't see those who shiver in some
distant alley, wander wretched in
the night or protest in voices grown hoarse
by begrudging time. He doesn't smell
their stench, isn't shamed by their demands.

Safe from disease, the menace of nature
or those who think they owe him one,
the latest technology allows him to visit
with family and friends via cyberspace.
But from time to time, curled up

with one of those first editions or admiring
the foolproof security of his home,
he wonders about the world out there,
remembers a field of wildflowers,
vaguely curious about the other half.

The Snake in My Dream

I know that snake, I have seen her
before: endless twists
of tensile tubing the color
of lemon Jell-O

resisting your outstretched arms
as you navigate a mountain trail,
its steep descent creating
a problem of balance.

One of those dreams that
continues to rage
long after waking. The snake
didn't seem to have a head

or tail or, if she did, the features
of each were interchangeable,
taunting me
to tell them apart.

Freud and his kind taught us
snakes symbolize sex,
ready as they always were
to define the category

in male terms. But this snake
was as unsexed
as the liquid effervescence of neon
in lightning bugs at dusk.

I beg the yellow snake to stop
invading my waking hours.
I tell her there'll be time enough
for further exploration

when I next dream her
frenetic body,
threatening to disarrange
my desert home.

But she has become a household
member now, the uninvited
guest destined to abuse
my comfort, divert my attention

from human violence, war,
destruction of habitat
and the other routine issues
murdering these times.

Rules of Engagement

This house has a sprained ankle,
that one a broken arm.
Accidents that happen in backyards
or on sidewalks
and never intentionally.

This house is allergic to spring,
summer, fall and winter.
Every season causes watery eyes,
feverish cheeks
and a runny nose.

This house isn't sick, just acts
that way, feels
she must explain herself in an era
of suspect symptoms
when everyone has a friend.

This house is afraid of COVID,
takes all the precautions,
has had all the shots.
Its life is pandemic-challenged
and changed.

This house suffers from
a rare condition
that could kill at any moment
or remain at bay
for years.

This house is terminally ill
but won't talk about
its misfortune.
It wants to enjoy the time
it has left.

None of these houses wishes
to be defined by sickness
but by health.
They all agree the rules
of engagement are wrong.

Home

The temperature inside these walls
is smug at times, edgy
at others. We have closed
the door, cleansed the air
of those toxins
attacking the lungs
and poisoning the mind.

Books that were forever
have been replaced
by those that fit
in a thousand square feet
or hide, embarrassed,
in digital devices almost
ashamed to speak their names.

Friends marveled that we hung
our walls with paintings
before arranging the furniture.
What we couldn't keep
went to museums, sharing
with a world that needs
the power of art.

Here is room for all we need:
workspaces—yours
and mine—surrounded
by invisible borders
like those electric fences
meant to keep small animals
in or out.

Here is the bed that receives
our different bodies
on a mattress that argues
the requirements of each,
finds the compromise
of what they
can endure.

Hotel-grade dinnerware
with the images
Mary Colter borrowed
from ancients who still
speak to us, a place to prepare
the food we eat and the place
we let it go.

We know we are fortunate
to have this home, warm
in winter, cool in summer heat,
this roof to protect
from weather's rage
and the violence
eroding our shores.

We open the only door
leading out
to invite those into our home
who also live
inside the circles of passion
and grief that sustain us
in these dangerous times.

If Forced to Go

If I had to pack an emergency bag
to have at the ready in case
of fire or flood, I would have to include
the big wall with your painting of swings,
one hundred books and this table
that welcomes friends to food
and conversation.

It would be hard to do without
our bed, that soft place
where I soiled a sheet in fever
and you washed it without a word,
where your nervous legs
eventually settle into
restful sleep,

scene of the love we make
and that which simply
surrounds and holds us
in its arms, aroused and safe
at the same time,
that place we belong
and that belongs to us.

My emergency bag would have
to be large enough to hold
this house with its hidden places
vast and small, all memories
past and present,
all objects solid and incorporeal
I'd want to take if forced to go.

This House

This room was once papered,
in a pattern of *Fleur de Lis*,
brown and gold against a background
darkening through the years
until one with the oak molding
lining exits and entryways.
The room closed its eyes but sleep

wouldn't come. Formal photographs
in loving frames left paler squares
when moved or replaced as new
baptisms and weddings, a honeymoon
in the Bahamas or backyard game of catch
found its way onto the family map
and stayed.

On the concave cushions of this couch
Bertie and Mildred snuck a caress
when her mother left the room
to refresh their pot of tea.
Hannah and Bess knew enough
not to risk the same
eighty years on.

In this room a sturdy four-poster
remembers Pa's last wheeze
and the sweat of Martha
who wanted a home birth
but didn't know her body's fluids
would live on
in its walnut frame.

Somewhere in the depths of this closet
is a Bible with births and deaths,
their dates inscribed
in careful penmanship,
dry leather flaking from a spine
that smells of camphor
and a litany of lies.

In this room of sweet potato pie
heirloom mixing bowls
never held anything but purest
chocolate mousse. And in 1913
Fred W. Wulf, he of Fort Wayne, Indiana
fame, invented the topknot
making its icebox a refrigerator.

Memory's cast-iron stove with its
compartment for stacked wood
was replaced by a Chambers Range
and then the five-burner model
with two ovens, pride
of the woman of this house
today.

The woman of this house today
was born in the wrong body
but finally arrives complete
through decision and courage,
embraced by a community
that believes we have the right
to our authentic selves.

If these rooms could speak, they'd tell
histories that make you laugh
and cry, reveal battles in our wars
of liberation, colors of change
and music that rouses us to futures
we cannot imagine but welcome
when they come.

Imposter Home

Their apartment stiffened its shoulders
when I arrived, shy bouquet of flowers
in hand, breath paralyzed
in my throat.

These were the maternal grandparents
I was supposed to love
but feared and hated with a revulsion
I didn't understand.

Not then, at least. Not until decades
beyond their deaths,
no questions possible, no demand
for answers left in me.

I remember his smile sharpened with the aim
of devious weaponry, impossible
battles I was forced to fight
despite my tender years.

I can see her now, moving to reposition
a cushion before its occupant
returned to settle again on its puffed surface,
disturb once more its pristine smile.

Theirs was the imposter home
where collateral damage
lay in wait for anyone brave
or careless enough to enter.

A Bright Place

He was the uncle who lived with his mother
until she died, agreeable grin beneath
a weight of heavy drapes and bookcases
never meant for anything but alphabetized titles,
gilt letters on ridged leather spines.

They said he *wasn't right in the head*, cited
the mysterious illness of his youth.
And he kept on smiling, loving his mother
and keeping company with the secrets
drugging him in hidden pain.

Dark paintings leaned precariously above
those who passed beneath them.
Muted colors were no colors at all.
But mostly it was that musty odor of lavender
and windows shut against the world.

When she finally died, he surprised us
with the woman he'd loved
those many years, married quickly
and took her to live in a cheerful place,
its windows open to the sun.

Home That Is a Life

The land came first, twenty acres
of desert and canyon
where water kept running away,
demanding they drill deeper
and, even then, playing
hide-and-seek with their need.

A plywood shed came next, protection
against the rawness of this place
they already loved. Summers
they slept in it as they pulled the money
they needed from unyielding earth
and monsoon luck.

Still young and strong, they roughed out
living room, kitchen, bedroom,
laid adobes layer upon layer,
sketched in a fireplace and finally
strawbale studios where they would
work, one beside the other.

Delight at the path of the redtail hawk
and mountain lion tracks
discovered one morning
as high-altitude sun thawed the ground
and their claim upon it. A stronger fence
kept their chickens safe.

Those years are decades now, scarred
by age and illness. They barter pieces
of themselves to be able to remain:
fix that grumbling toilet, install
electric heating where none is needed,
forced to do better than chance.

And they are here for the duration,
still marveling at his carved
woodwork, her tiles brightening
kitchen walls, their memories
singing in this pure New Mexico air,
a home that is a life.

The House as Serpent

Like a robust serpent,
each spring
neighbors got together
to help build
another room.

One stitched onto the last,
space for another child
or workplace
where projects
started and stopped.

An architect, his house
didn't conform
to a blueprint or subscribe
to the styles
then in vogue.

And she followed him,
the affable husband
everyone liked,
whose rhythms
set the pace.

When he died suddenly
in midlife
the last room
was only half finished,
caught in a gaping yawn.

She's over one hundred today
and that home
of her marriage and family
is a memory that comes to visit
only on friends' lips.

She doesn't know who lives
there now or if they have
straightened the angles, painted
over the lines that recorded
her children's growth.

That snake has become
a forgotten feature
on a landscape asleep in
stories built by gentle hands
and told by ghosts.

Adobe Dreams

Adobe dreams the heat of ancient summers
before earth worried a future
now breaking down all doors,
crawling through every open window.

Like those igloos carved from arctic ice,
home grows from what is:
place as possibility. Paper stretched across
a bamboo frame in Japanese restraint,

bison skins on the Great American Plains,
Iroquois Longhouse or Bucky's
geodesic dome. Highrise, penthouse,
tract, or starter home.

Ndebele's brightly painted abodes talk back
to a history of slavery's dismal canvas.
When Wright and Colter used local materials
it wasn't economy but elegance of vision,

oneness with a horizon that embraces
its settlers generously. From the cluster
of tents where those without homes
make do to a movement

of tiny homes where less is more
because it can be. *People who live
in glass houses shouldn't throw stones* isn't
about what we use to build our cocoons

but how we act once we dwell in them,
infusing our shelter with the energy
of each breath drawn, each word or gesture
that makes a house a home.

Dysfunctional Mirrors

The house stands mute on a hill
or set between replicas
on an ordinary block.

Glass bricks are dysfunctional mirrors
protecting and threatening
simultaneously.

A door may be heavy with locks
or hang an invisible sign
proclaiming *No Trespassing,*

power keeping you in line
and every face smiling,
every lie preserved.

What happens inside the house
stays inside
with Vegas vengeance.

The young girl may forgive
her father, forget his
ominous footsteps in the night

or remember when it's too late
for her but maybe she can
keep her daughter safe.

A house is only a home when
memory rides unhindered
one generation to the next.

The Treasure Hunt

When a house becomes a treasure hunt
we clean closets, go through drawers,
search photograph albums
with the determination of Nancy Drew
in her sensible shoes, flashlight
and magnifying glass at the ready.

Those who might answer our questions
are gone now, their secrets split
like atoms before such particles announced
their presence in curious minds, before
this race's baton could be passed
to reaching hands.

We are left to follow their last breaths into
dark basements and cluttered attics
where each box we open reveals
another clue but never the answers
we need as we travel lives
that are barely whispers now.

Rather than inflict this mystery upon
another generation of descendants
seeking to make the trouble
our world requires, I am writing
it all down, putting it in books
where it stays safe and willing.

When a house has become a treasure hunt
it no longer embraces the business
of everyday living
but bothers every room
with a nervous tic that proclaims:
Private Property – Do Not Enter.

My Memory's Houses

Nine Roosevelt Place or maybe Seven,
my childhood Scarsdale fades
along with its rigid mores and social rules.
But the ceiling trapdoor
in my bedroom closet still brings
a shudder, the space beneath the stairs
with my imaginary friends the sense
I could make my own belonging.

Driving along Albuquerque's narrow
Silver Avenue all these years
later, I don't remember it
on this side of Central. I am looking
for a plain box-like building,
the efficiency apartment
where a young bride had just
moved out of her parents' home.

A lifetime past, the memory
floating in its place is me
clutching a yellow seersucker robe
dodging the moves
of that pale-faced lecher
who collected the monthly rent.
His leering face,
my trembling revulsion.

Nineteen-fifties New York and home
was anything but efficient. Old
stairwell odor, old floorboards
painted gunmetal gray. Old walls.
Photos of immigrants
coming off a boat. Remnants
of the woman whose death
ushered me into that walkup.

Seventeen dollars bought furniture
from the Salvation Army store:
railroad flat with its army
of cockroaches, kitchen bathtub
and Ukrainian landlord's
translating daughter
who asked each month if I was sure
I could afford the rent.

That Lower East Side address
—428 East Ninth Street—
is etched in my memory
like a national holiday.
Where I lived my failures,
made my own mistakes,
finally embarked on this
precipitous journey to me.

In Mexico I purchased my first
real house, upstairs
and down, chicken coop
in the back patio,
bougainvillea tumbling over a fence
in front, family home we had to leave
when the paramilitaries
came to call.

In Cuba residence was awarded
according to family size,
furnishings taken from the homes
of a fleeing bourgeoisie.
Always more than a ninety-mile view,
windows salted open or shut
by years of sea air, cold water
when there was water at all.

Nicaragua brandished revolution
and five thousand dollars
got me a small house
on a quiet street
soon to become as dangerous
as any. Years later I couldn't
find my way back, struggled
to recognize its place in time.

And then I came home, closed
this circle opened so many
years before, returned to the desert
where a young woman was embraced
by red rock walls, the blooming arms
of cholla, wind-churned slivers of sand
biting my calves and a language
born on my tongue.

My parents built me a house
beside theirs, mountain trails
touching the entitled streets
of a neighborhood I finally left
when I could no longer
swallow its requirements
or feel at home
in its straitjacket of scorn.

You and I were together
by then, and you
had become my home.
Moving to our joined rhythms,
we surrounded ourselves
with courage, art, and all
that makes a house the place
where we may grow.

When do a roof and walls
become that map
of connective tissue?
One that protects
rather than projects
society's imposter image?
When do we arrive
to stay?

Words That Tell Our Story

I had only myself, struggling
to reimagine my time
as a place when I could live.

Then I gave birth for the first time,
in that moment becoming
more than the sum of my parts.

Second, third and fourth only added
to that sense of home
I carry with me as I go.

And you, love, recreate home
each morning we wake
together, each generous night.

On this side of life, with all of you
holding me up,
I know home is woven

of eyes that look back and up,
arms that reach out, words
that tell our story.

My Kitchens

I've had many. One in the middle
of a New York tenement flat,
tub beside sink, apartment-size
stove where I opened the oven door
for heat before the city mandated
radiators in every room.

Sitting around its thrift-shop table
I served my signature paella
to father and brother who barely
touched the robust peppers
and giant shrimp costing
a week's wages.

Other kitchens since that one,
larger and better endowed,
showed off their wooden
cutting boards, first appliances
purchased guiltily and enhancing
the magic of the feeding art.

Years of kitchens, some larger
some smaller, still teach me
accessories matter less
than craft and patience:
ingredients needed to create
what feeds every mouth.

Darkroom

My first was in Cuba, a tiny
maid's bathroom,
its fixtures long gone, not even
a door I could close.

Nine floors up, we hung a sheet
to mask the lights
of a city in shadows, washed
our prints in a stone washtub

when there was water, made
our chemicals from scratch
and gloried in what we created
from almost nothing.

In Nicaragua I had a better
start: water that ran
from faucets in the room itself
and, yes, a door.

It wasn't until I came home
to New Mexico
that I could build my darkroom
as I built my house:

to specification, with a system
that filtered toxins
from the air and gifted hours
of oblivion.

Then it ended, diagnosis of emphysema
killing the art I reveled in,
that place where I could lose myself
in dream.

My succession of darkrooms
lives in memory now,
still producing images from an eye
that sees.

What I Harvest

Morning opens its sleep-filled eyes,
deposits pink and orange
between the dark slats of
my bedroom blind, still closed
to resist the day.

If I raise the shade, this wall changes
from artichoke to lettuce green
and I notice the surfaces
are painted a progression
of hues.

Such range of light raises
the temperature
of my mind, these hours
I've spent on an idea
old as primal data.

Winter's frozen arms reach out
to pull me into its cave
of icicles, stalagmites
bruising my body with
their crooked fingers of pain.

The greens work as intended, wake
to keep me safe, hold me apart
from a world I don't want,
won't invite in or visit
in these treacherous times.

It's all about intensity of color,
slowed breath coming
to the rescue, planting its seed
at the hollow of my throat
and what I harvest there.

If These Walls Could Talk

If these walls could talk, alluding
to ideas before their time,
events unpublished or those hidden
for fear of stigma or shame.

In my childhood home Mom and Dad
walked naked through its rooms,
encouraged our questions,
answered as they could.

Yet they hid their secrets,
convinced themselves
we believed the stories they wove
from longings and from pain.

Like every child, I vowed I'd be
a different kind of parent,
tell my children the truth
no matter what the cost.

My walls hold their own secrets
and lies, their own narrative
woven of desire and need.
We are what is born of our truth

when we understand our parents
did the best they could
and we do our best for those
we hope will do it better.

Our Home Is No Center Court

We don't count chores
or measure duties.
Our home is no center court
where backhand contends
with a masterful serve
for points.

There is no chart tacked to
the refrigerator door
with colorful magnets,
assigning daily tasks
or weekly responsibilities
to each.

No one speaks about who
is expected to do what
in this space
we share with compassion,
generosity and
delight.

Here each sets her goals
at more than 100%,
doesn't limit herself
to a bottom line
or in any other way
betray our love.

Making a House a Home

There's a difference between strawbale
and straw, one the sophisticate's take
on raw materials, the other poverty's
solution.

Bamboo because it grows nearby
or bamboo the signature trend
of Japan's most prestigious
architectural firm.

Plaques of tin patchworked
as makeshift roof or tin
elegantly tooled by a master
in the art.

Where rebar emerges drunk and unruly
from unfinished structures
you know protection from the cold
is all there is.

Brick and mortar advertise building
with what will last,
looking beyond immediate
shelter.

In the ghettos of Mumbai, Rio and
New York, words like *upscale*
and *high end* aren't on any squatter's
lips.

The gauge is always running water,
electrical current, heat in winter,
and air where the tropics lay heavy
on your breath.

When famous architects put their names
on the plans, it's about more
than design and wood,
steel and glass.

No one imagines a solid gold
toilet will ever translate
into happiness or make a house
a home.

Lawn Signs

Almost all the houses on this block display
a belligerent lawn sign proclaiming
the criminal's name in red-white-and-blue,
advertisement by boast and patriotic colors,
while a single yard, defiant and proud,
speaks nonconformity.

Big business once paid struggling farmers
to let it paint *Drink Coca Cola*,
Elect Willis - He'll Work for You, or
Jesus Saves on the roofs of old barns,
their faded messages still quilt
a struggling countryside.

Today's signs don't offer cash but demand
payment from those who can't explain
their belligerent stand,
only know they fear neighbors' rejection
and follow the leader
onto this national gameboard.

I drive until I find the only sign that works
for me: *In this house we believe: Black Lives
Matter, Women's Rights are Human Rights,
No Human is Illegal, Science is Real,
Love is Love,
Kindness is Everything.*

The site of such sentiment is small, needs
paint and solidarity in this ugly time
when sleepwalking is easier
than honest discussion
and the art of listening
hides its face in anxious wait.

Feigning Ignorance

My house bleeds now
when I least expect
its wounds to release
such evidence of pain.

Its blood follows
no calendar,
reports no cycles
of the moon.

This hemorrhage tells
an old story
of wanton violence,
leaves a trail of tears.

If I could gauge its fever
I would find a history
of impoverished huts
fighting mansions,

their inhabitants feigning
ignorance of what
one must relinquish
for another to live.

My house bleeds and I try
to staunch its wounds
knowing I should
cleanse and cauterize.

We're all complicit
until we build
with compassion
as well as brick.

Something You Learned to Make

As a child, your house
had mother, father,
brother, sister, and dog.
And you had a room
but it never felt like yours
because you lived in dread
of what happened there.

What you needed: glasses
to see, but they said
they cost too much.
Ducks in a pond until
Dad shot them dead
with his .45 when they
quacked during one

of those dinners after you
all said grace, swallowed
the food, then trembled
before the surprise
that didn't surprise you
because you waited
for its obscenity.

You were always ready, a
condition that made you
sick. The big guy hit you
too, said it was his right.
Until one day when
you stared him down.
It ended then,

those moments I mean
but not their echo.
That was his gift for life,
a memory you didn't want
but learned to navigate
like a small boat balanced
upon a raging sea.

Your house had windows
and doors, a roof and
rooms where family lived,
but it wasn't a home.
Home is something else,
something you learned to make
once you had your own.

Homeless

Homeless we call them, as if
the designation carries
all that they are: those without
homes in this richest country,
sleeping in doorways
or seeking refuge in shelters
with more demand than beds.

Our language is so often
too small in this way,
names people for what
they lack rather than
the human complexity
that fills us all: identities
that do us proud.

Homeless we say, instead
of *those without*
a home at present, who
had one once and may
have one again
if luck and aid conspire
to change direction in their lives.

We live in a culture that defines
existence at its worst,
shies away from the
empathy that would let us
see wholeness beyond
that moment in time
when tragedy strikes its blow.

Survivor's Guilt

2020 started us on a journey:
home the only safe place
to be.

Beyond its familiar perimeter
unseen danger stalked
our every step.

Inside, we breathed the rarified
air of commercial promise,
meticulous guarantee.

We disinfected surfaces,
bought wholesale masks,
scrubbed our hands raw.

Two years have passed and we
emerge from quarantine
unsure.

Our bodies tell us they have
lost more than a willingness
to risk.

Our minds play strange tricks
as infection is mirrored
in imagination.

Faces are missing from this map
of friends, names have
been forgotten.

They say experience teaches
but I wonder if the virus
hasn't ushered in

a new definition of home:
survivor's guilt our
faithful companion now.

Where Does He Belong?

You might say this doesn't belong
in a poem, but I say
nothing is safe from stanzas
meant to grab and engage you
in the discourse of these times.

Men without homes relieve themselves
in the alley behind where we live
in modern apartments,
every need fulfilled, every
luxury at hand.

When I say relieve, I mean shit.
With nowhere else to go,
they take a shit by the dumpsters
in broad daylight and to the dismay
of those whose homes

are close enough to smell, see and
rage at such gross indignity.
One neighbor sends
daily letters, expressing
her disgust and impotence.

A few civic-minded folks suggest
getting together to rent
a porta potty, but no one volunteers
to stock it with paper
or keep it clean.

The undeclared war between those
who have homes and those
who don't is being waged right here
on this spot where human need
meets privilege.

You might tell me a homeless man
shitting up the neighborhood
doesn't belong in a poem,
but I ask you:
where does he belong?

The Word *Home* Is a Long Memory

If images endured millennia
would I see someone enter
or leave their cave? Chances
are, they carry fire
to light the space
they've chosen as home.

I want to ask her how she feels
at his side, him if he believes
he rules her and the children
multiplying his company:
their tiny open mouths,
their cries.

Is this a home that offers more
than shelter? Crude as it is,
can it provide order or nostalgia,
invisible barrier against
sky's random terror or wooly
mammoth's menacing tusk?

So much has changed from then
to now: most of us
build or buy our homes,
endow them with what
we are able in efficiency,
comfort, privilege.

The word *home* is a long memory
that cures our deepest wounds
and invites us to rejoice
until it leaves suddenly without
saying goodbye, doesn't look back
or give us a second thought.

My Home's Geometry

Within its rectangular perimeter
there is no straight angle,
no corner that isn't open
or closed beyond
suburban breath.

The rooms in our home
are a brilliant jigsaw
of irregular shapes,
floor plan accentuated
by queer horizons.

This feng shui energizes
more than wind
and water, balances us
with a secret element
imagined

by an architect whose name
isn't in the books,
neither revered nor
studied but breaking
every obstinate rule.

And the whole map curls
into a spiral leading us
to the heart of the matter,
where we may nest
and stretch.

Peach-Colored Blanket

In autumn the peach blanket
appeared on my bed,
its satin binding comforting
my quivering chin, its warmth
saving me from winter.

Without that peach blanket
the seasons couldn't have
unspooled themselves,
my calendar would have lacked
its marching orders.

Its comforting color, prologue
to comforting taste, peaches
soon became my favorite
fruit, moist texture of summer
on my lips.

The blanket, smelling faintly
of camphor—moths might
endanger its integrity—
was as much a feature
of my childhood

as Mother's Velveeta cheese
and overcooked vegetables,
Dad's bologna sandwiches
or Friday string quartets,
the dark colors

bathing my childhood home:
their consolation burying
the deeper contradictions
in earth I would only learn
to till in memory.

Whatever Its Name

You don't know you've lost it
until you find it again
or it finds you.

Chi, Prana, or simply the life force
that surges through
every living being.

After that assault of fevers
claiming my body
with relentless rage

tried to convince me it had
come for the duration,
my breath broke free.

I feel it now, lifting, making
me strong again
against the threat of all befores.

Buoyed by day and rocked asleep
at night, I am grateful
for this energy, whatever its name,

making its home in me—

Returning the Volley

They tell us age brings discomfort
if not disaster
and we must accept its limitations
to a supple body, ready wit.

In a dozen ways they emphasize
our diminished resources,
the slowed mind, the muscle
struggling to catch up.

And if words don't clue us in, all
we need do is observe them
speaking *about* rather than *to* us
in our presence.

Treated as children when we
were children was bad
enough. It inscribes a painful circle
now that we are old.

Until I no longer retain a throat
for laughter, a voice
that echoes this beating heart
and curious mind

I will return your volley of misplaced
darts and ignorant assumptions
with an aim propelled
by a life well lived.

Tomorrow's Temperature

Worries like overripe berries
fall about us, some rotted
beyond recognition,
some still holding
their lick of saccharine hope.

Earth, spreading her arms
in every season,
receives them all.
Our anxious feet bleed
their excess pain.

When sky darkens above us
and water evaporates,
dare to imagine a river
cascading over rocks
on some bold landscape.

The force of your dream
may shake loose
a bounty hidden in hope,
a resource that failed to show
her face before.

Those worries will still bother
your feet, spread flat
and cracked by time,
but future will rise in your eyes
bearing tomorrow's temperature.

Architecture

Before we recorded our history
in books that only lied
about the important things,
people dug into berms of earth
to shelter themselves.

Heat and cold were seasonal enemies
vanquished with hands
that burrowed. Space to gather
and eat around a cooking fire
was enough.

Slowly, curious minds imagined
timber cut from trees
and rocks or bricks shaped of clay
around openings to take in vistas
of the knowable world.

Architecture came later, a discipline
juggling art and commerce,
playing with pocketbook and taste:
plantation grandeur, adobe traditional
and their neighborhood codes.

A thousand identical homes marched
along the streets of Levittown
and Levittown West, opportunity for all
in a country that tells us
anyone can make it.

Community disintegrates to property value,
what makes some places desirable
while others fall beneath the stress
of poverty. Who moves in
and who cares.

A Black family lives in the corner house.
The roar of motorcycle engines
sounds on a once-quiet block.
Who knows what those two women
are up to in 3711?

It's no longer simply a matter of shelter,
warmth and comfort, but a code
of conduct anything but compliant
with human need
and the real hunger of living.

Where We Create What We Make and Do

Foundations count in houses
as in people. They must
go deep and strong
to support
what rises above.

Where the earth trembles
and quakes,
buildings are meant
to sway, not break,
dance rather than fall.

Where sun is strong all year,
we harness it
for heat. Where rain
floods, we pay attention
to the roof.

Walls with high windows
have room for art
while those with large ones
frame the art of nature's
magical seasons.

There may be a bedroom for her
and one for him
but in the happiest homes
they sleep together. Two women
almost always share.

The kitchen can feature
shiny appliances
but those that feed best
embrace a table
set for guests and family.

Still, those rooms that take
the deepest breaths
and sing loudest
are where we create
what we make and do:

that which gives energy
to a home, this
collection of rooms
where more than living
happens.

Going Home

They grasp her tired hand
and tell her
she's going home,
going to a place
where there is no pain
and she'll spend
eternity with God.

A litany of forgiven sins
and pleadings
with a Creator who listens
to millions of requests
from millions
of hungry mouths
and hopeful hearts.

No matter the story
is invention
from start to finish,
relief created as panacea
to calm the person dying
and comfort those
left behind.

Cultures from antiquity
to now have
devised such beliefs
to keep the faithful
in check,
exercise power
or give solace.

Unwilling to play protagonist
in a script based on lies,
I say believe
if that's what you need
to fabricate fact
and fantasy,
but leave me out.

What We Can Pretend We Do Not See

From the outskirts of town
you can see one hundred miles
on a clear day, no smoky air
lying in wait
to override the view.

On the fringes, smaller homes
wander along dirt roads
needing windows, a door,
and other improvements
only money can buy.

The childless couple with
a home on the hill
pays someone to clean
their empty bedrooms, change
the water in their pool.

The immigrant family shares
two bedrooms
with cousins who made it
across a barbed-wire border
fleeing thirst and dogs.

The home that gnaws at my conscience
is no home at all
but a dangerous street
where weather and violence
assault by turns.

Ours is a belligerent architecture
of property and taunt:
what we are willing to look at
and what we can pretend
we do not see.

Faked Orgasms and Beloved Books

A bedroom no longer remembers
faked orgasms or beloved books
read by lamplight on a night table
graced by memorabilia.

Living room has lost its portraits
of family gatherings, evenings
meant to impress a boss
or hide a high-school kiss.

Kitchen has forgotten its favorite
recipes. Too little salt in the
soup, excess of sugar
coating the tongue with regret.

Studio's hand trembles now when
it tries to apply paint to paper,
its writer's mind believes it will find
the lost word but doesn't.

Fireplace mantel cannot name
the trophies once parading
across its polished wood,
boasting triumph over will.

Even the attic, accustomed to boxes
of keepsakes stored for a rainy day,
has forgotten what lives
in its corners, carries its name.

Front door cannot say who entered
here, back door doesn't recall
who left. This house struggles
with dementia, tries hard

to pretend *it's all good*, rehearses
its answers, hoping those
who live between its walls
won't abandon its loving arms.

The Houses Are Full of People

Not the size of each house
that has given me home,
not the neighborhood
or number of rooms. Nothing
material worth a poem.

No front door grandeur, porch
or entryway. Kitchen
endowed with the latest appliances,
double-oven stove or one
that burns wood, coal, kerosene.

Nothing an architect or designer
could create, no vast acreage
or thirty-year mortgage
means anything on the checklists
where I've lived.

It's the people, the people alone
who fill those generational
stage sets where they played
as children, battled adolescent
angst, navigated separation.

They go out into their worlds,
the DNA of those homes
in their cells, warm memories
and harsh dismemberment
for the houses they will build.

Burdened by Unvanquished Greed

Perhaps we will birth solutions
to meet the demands
of so much willful ignorance.

They may be better equipped
to endure fire and flood,
resist the bilge of our absurdity.

They may win architectural prizes
at times when imagination
is forced to disregard desire.

When earth's temperature rises
past the tipping point,
will we inhabit caves once more

or leave our tired planet behind
and try again on the Moon,
still burdened by unvanquished greed?

Slow Growth

In the backwaters of a California
mountain range, Bristlecone
pines survive
four and a half millennia.

Their twisted trunks present
unexpected swirls,
changing directions
in such a wealth of seasons.

Scientists tells us the Bristlecone
only grows one inch
per hundred years, slow progress
mirroring determination.

How might a house of Bristlecone
respond to the needs of those
who dwell in its rooms, breathe
the scent of its wood?

We may never know because
the tree resists logging,
stands proud in its secret forest
where hikers try to find

Methuselah or other grandiose
specimens, their search
aimed at destruction
or perhaps only memory.

A Bristlecone house might last
a thousand years. We
are not testing longevity
but honoring metaphor.

More Than the Sum of Its Parts

This house blinks unobtrusively
when no one is looking
or makes an exuberant show
of its nervous tic.

Light breaks from its two big eyes
and all the little ones,
betraying locations long hidden
in attic or basement.

It stands on ballet toes, stretching
long legs that lift it above
the reach of hurricane
or flood.

It undulates arms devoid of wrists
and elbows, limbs that
can dance to the wild beat
of its booming heart.

A long thick braid descends
from its highest balcony
to the garden below, a ladder
unfurled for any escape.

When it makes music, this house
strikes only the black keys
on its piano, the lament it learned
from the pain of slaves.

This house shouts and laughs
and cries with the seasons,
singing itself to sleep each night
with a lullaby first heard

in the depths of a kitchen cabinet
way back behind the flour sifter,
enamel white with a cluster
of painted red cherries.

And this house has a tell, touches
its right cheek with left hand's
sweep of fingertips before it can
stop itself.

If a whole is forever more than
the sum of its disparate parts
this house is a puzzle still waiting
to be solved.

The Risk of Staying or Leaving

Heat might be the first to go
though a makeshift stove
tries its best.

A window no longer closes,
its broken seam rattling
in every storm.

Paint peeling from walls
reveals strange patterns,
forgotten colors.

When roof becomes unreliable
the stringent smell of tar
invades our lungs.

Foreclosure enters our speech
like a pushy relative
with nowhere else to go.

The old neighborhood hurts,
its properties betraying
all Monopoly boards.

When a beloved house
is no longer a home
we are faced with the risk

of staying or the risk of leaving,
neither road sign nor map
to show us the way.

All It Took

My childhood home was not concerned
with how I addressed it:
residence or *nest, pad* in the lingo
of the day.

Once satisfied with *Craftsman*, *Ranch*,
Tudor or *Greek Revival*,
those places we inhabit have become
more personal now.

Home today requests I distinguish
between *Him*, *Her*, or *They*,
not wanting to limit itself to
any architectural symmetry.

And don't think you can tell by looking.
The rugged log cabin may not
be *Him* but come from a kit
assembled on site.

The Cape Cod Cottage with flowered
curtains and white picket fence
is no more *Her*
than the lipstick lesbian.

They enjoys an identity you must plumb
to understand, sweeps their closets
clean of lies
and other impediments.

In just my lifetime we have gone from
Mrs. to *Ms.* and to the singular *They*.
All it took was a willingness to listen,
nothing more.

The Animal of My House

My house is an elephant,
whose giant heart
goes back generations,
surprising me
with ancestral recall.

But not all that happened
then deserves applause
today. Some things
are better
buried in denial.

My house plays dinosaur,
making small boys laugh
and scientists scratch
their heads
in wonder.

My house displays the slow
and ponderous pace
of a Galápagos tortoise,
ancient in wisdom,
winner of any race.

Proud eagle's image appears
on a tortilla,
attracting the devout
in droves, mystifying
children.

My house is a dog, the
companion known
for its faithfulness
even when refusing to fetch
upon command.

Mine is a newborn kitten,
curled into its private
ball of fur, prepared
to be distant or secretive
by turn.

And mine is a caged canary
singing for its freedom
while feigning resignation
in a world where we dare
to say *it is what it is.*

That canary is happier
than a parrot trained
to mimic a litany of words
it's forced to repeat
for its supper.

My house is a boa squeezing
the air from anyone
destined to live between
its walls: *breathless* no longer
a benign adjective.

Or a rattler announcing itself
seconds before it strikes,
always taking more
than it gives and promising
nothing in return.

Who knows? My house
might be any snake
in tall grass, ready to
prevent home invasion
before it happens.

The animal of my home only
reveals itself to those
who master three-dimensional chess
or otherwise live
outside the envelope.

You Must Build Your Own Home

For my great granddaughter,
Julia Randall Esteche,
born October 13, 2022.

Tender One, you were born
into a home
shaped like the halves
of a single beating heart.

Its simple floorplan
is now the world
where your journey
of discovery begins.

Daughter of artists, you will
have the power of light
and color, solutions
others will not see.

In your mother's milk
you savor
the sweet memory
of overcoming.

Your father's gentle hands
beat the drum
that lulls you to sleep
each night.

Art is a coyote sibling, strong
but quirky foundation
for what you will
encounter as you go.

But, like the rest of us, you must
build your own home,
raise its walls, sweep
its rooms of unwanted secrets

and welcome the morning sun
through its windows.
You will open and close
your door on stormy days

and when least expected you'll be
the adult holding a newborn
whose unfocused eyes
search for yours.

Ancestral Curiosity

Do we define home by the things
it contains:
woven shirts in my closet,
clay bread pans exuding the scent
of thirty years of loaves,
books I reread with every season
and those I write,
washed sheets on a bed
where the imprints of our bodies live?

This floor, reliable
beneath my feet.
These walls embracing me
in calm and weather.
Roof of protective pride.
Windows and doors
like that strand of wool
leading beyond the border
of the Diné rug, imagining escape.

Holographic memory dances
in mirrors
that give back images of the child
afraid of what threatened
from the other side of her bedroom closet's
trap door, the woman who understands
freedom may come late
but brings stories
enough for the duration.

Home speaks a new language,
words we may
or may not understand,
translation hiding in a grove
of aspens, then emerging
to startle when you least expect.
We will always pronounce it
with an accent reminiscent
of ancestral curiosity, dogged chance.

This Table

This table's polished pine
remembers a forest
where young men and women
hide behind massive trunks:
Davids facing Goliath.

I set its surface with dishes
also hewn from the earth,
place forks to the left
of each setting, knives
and spoons to the right.

I ask the table to support elbows
of family and friends,
food in its daily rhythm,
conversation about that war
closing in on our home.

When the staccato of gunfire
and moans of the dying
are at a distance we believe
ourselves safe. The table
knows nothing and everything

about war, inequality, and grief,
trade routes that take
more than they give
and celebrate survival
only when every choice is spent.

Non-Negotiable

My home is a cavern of heartbeats
scaling its innermost walls
like a rock climber placing his toes
in the subtlest cracks.

My home is an ocean of slave ships
and shipwrecks but also
dolphins and whales
cresting the waves.

My home is rich in questions, forged
by the wonder of each generation
as it takes its place
at the table.

My home considers *need to know*
when it talks to me,
teaches me the power of patience
and resilience.

My home says shame is the only thing
it will not allow to cross
its threshold. *Non-negotiable*, it says,
and folds its arms.

The House as a Poem

I hesitate before placing
a comma or period
at the end of this corridor,
wonder if it all ends
here or if a promise
of ongoing argument
is hiding in the wings.

Like an opening stanza,
the entry initiates
my storyline, sets the stage
for family quarrels
and generational love,
contains the bashful seeds
of what's to come.

And stanza means room
in Italian, the part
of the poem like the room
in a house
where something happens
even when
it remains unseen.

Here we take a sharp turn
away from what we
expected next, acknowledging
life holds surprises
although every idea
was carefully tested,
studied in full.

A single preposition
can change
a color scheme,
make the difference
between good and great
in this literature
of place.

Nouns are obvious, standing
front and center as they do,
dressing for Sunday dinner
or sunbathing nude
in a backyard
for neighbors
peering over the wall.

Verbs demand more respect.
They are the weight-bearing
beams supporting
this structure's intimate secrets,
what may escape
an open window or door
that was left ajar.

Where you least expect
your culture of living
to honor tradition,
courage may present
the surprise ending
that alters
everything.

Margaret Randall (b. New York, 1936) is a poet, essayist, oral historian, translator, photographer, and social activist. She lived in Latin America for twenty-three years (in Mexico, Cuba, and Nicaragua). From 1962 to 1969, she and Mexican poet Sergio Mondragón co-edited *El Corno Emplumado / The Plumed Horn*, a bilingual literary quarterly that published some of the best new literature and art of the sixties. She is the author of more than two hundred books.

When she came home in 1984, the government ordered her deported because it found some of her writing to be "against the good order and happiness of the United States." With the support of many writers and others, she won her case in 1989.

Randall's most recent poetry titles include *Against Atrocity*, *Out of Violence into Poetry* (both from Wings Press), *Stormclouds Like Unkept Promises*, and *Vertigo of Risk* (both from Casa Urraca Press). A second volume of selected poems, *Time's Language II: Selected Poems 2019-2023*, was recently published by Wings Press. *Che on My Mind* (a feminist poet's reminiscence of Che Guevara, published by Duke University Press), *Thinking about Thinking* (essays, from Casa Urraca), and *Artists in My Life* (New Village Press) are other recent titles. In 2020, Duke published her memoir *I Never Left Home: Poet, Feminist, Revolutionary*.

She has also devoted herself to translation, producing *When Rains Become Floods* by Lurgio Galván Sánchez and *Only the Road / Solo el camino*, an anthology of eight decades of Cuban poetry (both published by Duke), among many other titles.

Randall received the 2017 Medalla al Mérito Literario, awarded by Literatura en el Bravo in Ciudad Juárez, Mexico. In 2018 she was awarded the "Poet of Two Hemispheres" prize by Poesía en Paralelo Cero in Quito, Ecuador. In 2019 she was awarded an honorary doctorate of letters from the University of New Mexico, and in 2022 she received the City of Albuquerque's Creative Bravo Award.

Randall lives in Albuquerque with her partner (now wife) of more than thirty-seven years, the painter Barbara Byers, and travels extensively to read, lecture, and teach.

Casa Urraca Press

Casa Urraca Press publishes creative nonfiction, poetry, photography, and other works by authors we believe in. New Mexico and the US Southwest are rich in creative and literary talent, and the rest of the world deserves to experience our perspectives. So we champion books that belong in the conversation—books with the power, compassion, and variety to bring very different people closer together.

We are proudly centered in the high desert somewhere near Abiquiú, New Mexico. Visit us at casaurracapress.com for exquisite editions of our books and to register for workshops with our authors.